Bears

Dona Herweck Rice

A bear has a snout.

A bear has a tail.

A bear has ears.

A bear has eyes.

A bear has paws.

A bear has claws.

A bear has fur.

A bear has teeth.

A bear has a growl!

Consultant
Jamey Acosta, M.S.Ed.
Reading Specialist and English Learner TOSA

Publishing Credits
Rachelle Cracchiolo, M.S.Ed., *Publisher*
Emily R. Smith, M.A.Ed., *SVP of Content Development*
Véronique Bos, *VP of Creative*

Image Credits: all images from iStock and/or Shutterstock

Library of Congress Cataloging-in-Publication Data
Names: Rice, Dona, author.
Title: Bears / Dona Herweck Rice.
Description: Huntington Beach, CA : Teacher Created Materials, 2025. | Audience: Ages 4-8 | Summary: "You can tell a bear by what it has. You can tell a bear by what it does, too!"-- Provided by publisher.
Identifiers: LCCN 2024039312 (print) | LCCN 2024039313 (ebook) | ISBN 9798765997284 (paperback) | ISBN 9798765997314 (ebook)
Subjects: LCSH: Bears--Juvenile literature.
Classification: LCC QL737.C27 R5155 2024 (print) | LCC QL737.C27 (ebook) | DDC 599.78--dc23/eng/20240826
LC record available at https://lccn.loc.gov/2024039312
LC ebook record available at https://lccn.loc.gov/2024039313

TCM Teacher Created Materials
5482 Argosy Avenue
Huntington Beach, CA 92649
www.tcmpub.com
ISBN 979-8-7659-9728-4